GLOOM, DOOM, AND VERY FUNNY MONEY

GLOOM, DOOM, AND VERY FUNNY MONEY

By Neil Innes
Illustrated by Richard Robinson

Piccadilly · London

Phototypeset by Goodfellow & Egan, Cambridge,
Printed and bound by WBC Ltd.,
for the publishers, Piccadilly Press Ltd.,
5 Castle Road, London NW1 8PR

A catalogue record for this book is available
from the British Library

ISBN 1-85340-134-X (hardback)
ISBN 1-85340-139-0 (trade paperback)

Neil Innes *lives in Suffolk, and is a well-known broadcaster, writer, and performer – in short a 20th Century Renaissance Man, and reluctant style guru. A fine arts graduate, he was a founder member of the Bonzo Dog Doo Dah Band.*

Richard Robinson *lives in North London, and is a well-known puppeteer. Recently, he has written and developed the Puddle Lane and Riddlers series for ITV. A graduate in psychology, he was the director of the Covent Garden Community Theatre.*

CONTENTS

This book is dedicated to Robin,
my long-suffering bank manager.

Introduction

Economics is called 'the dismal science'. Why? Because it doesn't seem to go anywhere or get anything done. It is always hanging around – like a younger brother or sister – stopping us having fun!

It is tedious because it is never-ending – it goes on and on. It is all about naming things, measuring things, and then giving the 'measurements' names.

It is all about robbing Peter to pay Paul – or in the case of Robert Maxwell, robbing Peter AND Paul in order to rob just about everyone else!

It is about everything and nothing – it cannot explain everything and it can ignore nothing.

To understand it fully is beyond even the best human brains. To understand it a little should be enough for most people – and the more people who understand it a little, the more useful it can be.

Like being able to tell the time, we don't have to be able to grasp the concept of infinity in order to turn up at 2.30 on a Saturday for a football match.

I started writing this book believing it would be useful to halfwits like me who didn't understand the first thing about governments and big business.

I soon discovered that economics is not just all about money, it is all about human nature as well.

Seen through the eyes of economics, human nature is mostly self-interest, swiftly followed by greed, panic, and the primitive urge to throw stones at what we don't understand.

After a lifetime of ignorance, and lobbing the odd pebble, I found economics fascinating – and I hope you do too.

1

FUNNY MONEY!

WHAT IS MONEY?

'A fool and his money are soon parted', the old proverb warns us, and like the more modern saying: 'There is no such thing as a free lunch', both suggest there is more to money than meets the eye.

Nowadays, even the best things in life cost money – and whereas once we *used* money, money now seems to use us. Why? History has shown us that money can be anything!

Today, most of us think of money as coins, banknotes, plastic cards, or bank cheques, but in the past, it has also been feathers, stones, beads, and even shells.

Money can be any object that people believe is valuable. That's the important bit. What made all these wildly different things acceptable as money was that they were all an agreed and recognized means of payment.

This also applies to the invisible money that is stored in bank computer records which, even though you can't see it or touch it, can be used to buy things in the same way as any other form of money.

In other words, very simply, money is an idea.

BORN TO SHOP

But how did the idea of money come about? No one really knows, but there is little doubt that people learned to count before they could read and write, and the use of money was widespread long before written history.

It is also clear that the idea of money was invented out of necessity. As the early settlements developed and people had more and more valuable goods and skills to exchange, basic swapping could be quite complicated.

Just imagine, if you had a spare sheep and really wanted say, the very latest in loincloths, it could take you a very long time to find someone with the trendiest loincloths who *actually* wanted one of your sheep.

"WELL, THE GOOD NEWS IS, I MANAGED TO GET HER TO KNOCK A BIT OFF THE PRICE..."

So, in order to make all kinds of exchanges or trade easier, people soon saw the need for some sort of token that could represent or hold the value of whatever it was they had to exchange.

THE GO-BETWEEN

People needed something of value that they could take in exchange for whatever goods or skills they had to sell.

They could then give the same stuff to another person in exchange for something they might want to buy, or they could simply hold on to it – as a way of possessing something valuable.

Later on they realized it was better if it was small, easy to carry, and easy to divide. It was also better if it could be something that didn't fall to pieces after a lot of people had handled it.

ON THE ISLAND OF YAP IN THE PACIFIC, PEOPLE USED BIG ROUND STONES TO MAKE SOCIAL PAYMENTS AND SETTLE DISPUTES. THIS 'MONEY' COULD MEASURE UP TO 4 M ACROSS!

"COULDN'T WE TOSS SOMETHING OTHER THAN A COIN"

The original idea of money was marvellously simple. It worked! It was the best thing *before* sliced bread. It was a genuine means to an end, and that end was to simplify the day-to-day distribution and exchange of all the things that people really needed or otherwise considered worth having.

VALUE FOR MONEY

A commodity is something of use or advantage to mankind and, therefore, something of value. Since money was invented to make the exchange of commodities easier, it naturally follows that money would soon become valuable in itself – and no longer the simple go-between it once was.

Thanks to money, every commodity now has a price – the cost in money of something of value – and prices have always depended on supply and demand, and so has the value of money.

THE AGE-OLD DOUBLE-ACT – SUPPLY AND DEMAND

Supply is what we make or do, and demand is what we need or want. For example, if something is scarce – like food after a bad harvest – then prices will be high, because everybody needs food.

If, however, someone is daft enough to make a vast quantity of unbreakable pots, pretty soon the price of those pots will go down – because no one needs to replace them.

It is the same with basic money. Too much gold or silver – and too few commodities in the market place – can also mean the prices of goods and services going up, or, being able to buy *less* for your money – high prices.

On the other hand, plenty of goods for sale and too little money – and the precious metal would be more valuable – you could buy *more* for your money – low prices. So the value of money also depends on its own supply and demand.

YOU ASKED FOR THAT.

The demand for money is obvious – everybody needs it to buy the things they want. But who supplies it? Where does it come from? Wealthy people? People who control the money supply? Where do they get it from?

If we go back to first principles, someone must have owned something of value that someone else wanted and got given some money for it in exchange.

The money could then be used to produce even more goods – and provided there was still a demand, they could make even more money. Then, perhaps, someone with an army came along and stole all the money from them – who knows? Great wealth has been sloshing around the place for thousands of years – passing from one empire to another as each in turn saw its own rise and fall.

HOLDING THE PURSE STRINGS

Money came to be used as a measure of the value of other things, but it is quite important to remember that, at first, money could be anything so long as people believed it was worth having.

Well, having said that money could be *anything*, obviously it could not grow on trees for any casual passer-by to pick at random, so the first governments, or Tribal Chiefs, Kings, Pharaohs, Nabobs, whoever, had to decide what was valuable and then control the money supply – usually by collaring most of it for themselves!

As long ago as 4000 BC, more or less everybody using money agreed that the metals, silver, gold, and copper – in that order – were the most valuable.

Soon after, small amounts of the precious metals were accurately weighed and used as money. Coins with the official stamp or, more often, the portrait, of Rulers, came much later.

As time went by, more and more people began to want money for its own sake – for the power, status, influence, and, of course, security that having lots of it gave them over people without it.

Controlling the money supply was, and still is, the most important job in any society or civilization. But surely, it's not just the money that people are after, it's what the money can buy that we *really* want. Either way, the idea of money seems to be here to stay. Can you imagine a world without it?

MONEY SUPPLY, AND DEMAND

2

PIE IN THE SKY

WHAT IS ECONOMICS?

Most of us spend our lives balancing what we earn with what we would like to spend. Economics touches every part of our lives and yet most of us are complete halfwits when it comes to understanding what goes on. However, understanding something usually depends on how you look at it.

Take, for example, a football match. To someone not particularly interested in football, it is 22 men running around a field after a ball – they may also be dimly aware of the referee and the linesmen.

To the passionate football fan, however, there are two opposing teams, each made up of strikers, mid-fielders, defenders, and a goal-keeper. There are rules, tactics, and hopefully GOALS!

There are leagues of teams, managers, transfer fees, special pages in newspapers, interviews with star players who can be 'over the moon' or 'sick as a parrot' – it is the same with economics. Once you know the basic rules, everything else falls into place.

CREATIVE ACCOUNTANTS – FIRST ELEVEN

WHAT'S IN A NAME?

So what is economics anyway? As the name suggests, it is to do with all forms of economy – 'the management of expenditure' – from basic house-keeping to the theoretical science of the laws of production and distribution of wealth.

OK, that's a bit of a mouthful, but when words are taken one at a time, what they generally *mean* is simple enough.

(The Greek word *ecos* – meaning house, together with the suffix – *nomy* – which relates to law and distribution, gives us the 'modern' word *economy*.)

A hundred years ago, Alfred Marshall said that 'economics is merely the study of mankind in the ordinary business of life.' In other words, supply and demand – with money and human nature somewhere in between. Easy! So far so good . . .

More recently, John Kenneth Galbraith has refined Marshall into – 'economics is the study of the way people are organized for economic tasks by corporations, by trade unions and by government.'

Oh dear! But don't be alarmed – an economic task is simply whatever we do when we earn or spend money – at work or play. How we are organized – is how we sell our labour and skills and how we buy the things we need or otherwise value.

In their own long-winded way, today's economists are mainly concerned with the *valuation* of everything. So where did they get their ideas from?

WHO STARTED IT?

In the past, it was bishops and kings who made value judgements, not economists. Apparently, the power and wealth of the merchants and their mercantilism – trade or commerce – put an end to all that.

By the beginning of the sixteenth century, the Portuguese had gone all over the place and Columbus had discovered America and world trade suddenly expanded so rapidly that the value of money, above all other things, began to undermine the power of both church and throne.

Around this time, scholars began writing down what could be described as the first theories of economics.

In 1515, only 23 years after Columbus had opened the door to the South American gold and silver mines, Thomas More, son of a merchant, published his book, *Utopia*.

Full of moral values and no nonsense from land-owning nobility, Thomas More advocated the complete abolition of private property as the only cure for the 'poverty, hardship, and worry' of the 'vast majority of the human race'.

He further rejected money as a domestic currency – gold and silver were for trading with foreigners – because he preferred to believe in natural, innocent behaviour, all too easily corrupted by the presence of money as the only thing of value.

Necessities and comforts, not luxuries, were all that was to be consumed in Utopia; everyone would share equally in a common wealth. Merchants would unite with labourers and craftsmen against aristocrats and goldsmiths (who were in the process of becoming the first bankers).

Thomas More sided against the nobility in the great class struggle which was dividing people all over Europe.

AND IN THE BLUE CORNER . . .

In stark contrast, 150 years later, Thomas Hobbes deduced that there must be an unquestionable sovereign power for any society to survive.

In his book *Leviathan,* he assumes that hostility between individuals is inevitable as they struggle for their own ends.

Leviathan describes a society where the fear of being poor forces all to compete for wealth and only a really strong authority can maintain any civil order.

Only the Sovereign should have the absolute right to distribute and redistribute the means of production among subjects – especially land and international trading opportunities. No wonder they had a civil war and chopped the King's head off!

POURING OIL ON TROUBLED WATER

By the eighteenth century, the 'Age of Enlightenment', Adam Smith had declared firstly, that self-interest guides people to serve the *common* interest as though by an invisible hand.

Secondly, that competition in each line of business or trade not only regulates market prices, it also sets them.

Thirdly, thanks to competition, there was no reason for the state to interfere in the market place. All a government had to do was keep law and order and defend the country.

Lastly, since competition and the market brought the best results – more money for everyone – Smith advocated there should be as much of both as possible. The bigger the trading area, the more competition, and therefore, the stronger the market.

This was the first argument for free trade and also the founding or 'classical' design of an economy.

SEARCHING FOR THE IDEAL STATE -
THE DIALOGUE CONTINUES....

It may also be worth noting that 1776, when Adam Smith wrote *The Wealth of Nations*, was also the year in which the Americans fought and won their War of Independence – and that the French Revolution was only just around the corner.

THE NEVER-ENDING STORY

Smith's ideas were gradually refined by other economists, into the neo-classical economies of the industrialized countries like the United States, Britain, Germany, and France at the beginning of the twentieth century.

So, like football fans, it would seem that economists can disagree in theory about many aspects of their science or art and, while they may agree on *where* they disagree, they hardly ever agree on *why* they disagree.

However, to the innocent bystander or economic halfwit, *why* they disagree is perfectly obvious – it is purely political – and since the world is populated by people with differing self-interests and therefore different political solutions – why should economists be any better than the rest of us?

They too, have to earn a living and all sorts of economists are employed to interpret what is happening to money in the way that most favours the various interests of their employers.

If things are looking bad, very often government economists will advise politicians to be '*economical*' with the truth – and why not? People are basically nervous and insecure, and given that money plays a part in everything we do, telling people how bad things really are could only make matters worse!

THE TRIUMPH OF OPTIMISM

"GOOD NEWS, FELLOWS! THIS CBI REPORT SAYS THE **INCREASE** IN THE **ACCELERATION** OF **BUSINESS GLOOM** IS **LEVELLING OUT!**"

3

LENDING AND BORROWING

SNEAKY TRICKS!

Money can be anything. It is after all, only a medium of exchange, something to lubricate the mighty cogs of trade – (and also the hinges of doors in the corridors of power!) – so why did we change from using gold and silver as money?

Why do we use the elaborately printed paper notes and the coins of harder metals today?

When coins were made of the softer precious metals – and things were literally 'worth their weight in gold' – many dishonest people found it easy to take the precious metal coins, clip small bits off and melt the cuttings down for themselves.

Others mixed less-precious metals in with the silver or gold and effectively debased or made the coins less valuable – so eventually all people with money, mostly governments, and merchants – had to look for somewhere to keep it safely, in a place of deposit.

So, since the public at large could not be trusted with the 'real' money, alternatives had to be found.

It is believed that the Chinese were the first to introduce the idea of paper money. However, as more and more governments began isssuing paper notes equal to the value of their 'precious metal' coins – it was quickly discovered that more 'notes' could be issued than there were coins!

This was because most people were quite happy to carry the paper around with them and not try to cash it in – so long as they were fairly certain they could get the *real* money if they tried.

Of course, the extra notes the governments issued increased the money supply and, to their delight, paid the governments bills just as well as silver or gold. If prices went up, so what? The 'powers that be' could afford to lower taxation – and still stay relatively popular with the ordinary folk!

This sort of thing has been going on ever since and when, in the Great Depression of the 1930s, so many people wanted gold instead of cash, the internationally agreed European 'Gold Standard' of 1867 had to be abandoned.

THE FIRST BANKS

The first private banks were the goldsmiths because they had the best strongboxes. Very soon the banks discovered that they could lend these 'deposits' to someone else and charge interest.

Interest is a charge for borrowing money, usually a percentage of the amount borrowed. If you borrow £10,000 at a rate of interest of 10% for one year, you pay back £11,000 at the end of that year. The lender has made money – £1,000!

But, more importantly, the 'real' money didn't have to leave the bank. The borrower was given notes certifying that he had the amount of the loan in the bank. He could then use the notes for whatever he wanted to buy.

The original depositor still had his money, the borrower also had 'money' and the bank, by making the loan, had *created* money and thus increased the money supply as well as making a profit on the interest!

And so it is today, except of course, that we no longer use gold or silver to 'value' our money. Money is created by the lending banks under the control of the central banks which in turn, with the notable exception of Germany, are controlled by governments.

Out of the £1,000 interest earned by the bank, it will, maybe, invest £250 in something not too risky that will not only earn the bank interest – but also be fairly easy to turn into cash again.

INTEREST

SO, MARCO, YOU WANT TO DISCOVER CATHAY – THAT'S INTERESTING!
GOLD

NOTES INSTEAD OF GOLD – THAT'S ... UM ... INTERESTING!
PROMISE TO PAY ONE POUND OF GOLD

2 YEARS LATER
A NINE HUNDRED PERCENT RETURN ON THE INVESTMENT – THAT'S VERY VERY VERY INTERESTING!
GOLD
AND I NEVER LEFT THE BOX – THAT'S FASCINATING!

This leaves £750 to lend to other people.

This is how the system works. From each £100 of new deposits, the bank will keep £10 and lend £90 to someone who wants to buy, let's say, a new suit. The borrower buys the suit and gives the money to the tailor.

The tailor puts the £90 in *his* bank which will then keep £9 and lend £81 and so on, and so on. Since the money eventually finds its way back into the banking system, out of each £100 of deposits, £1,000 of spending power is available to the economy.

THE WAY THE MONEY GOES ...

MONEY MAKES MONEY

More and more people are paying money to borrow more and more money, and more and more people are finding more and more ways of making money out of lending even more money. All rather confusing really . . . or is it?

People who own money like it to work for them. By saving, or depositing their money with a bank or building society they will earn interest and in turn the bank or building society will also earn interest from lending the savers' money to someone else.

Money can also be 'earned' by buying commodities or goods which are expected to rise in value or, it can be invested in government bonds or company stocks and shares. Whatever the method or risk, the money, profit, or capital gain that is made by using other money is called a return.

For each way of using money to make more money – there is a money market – and just as you would expect with something as imaginary as money, each market is not a 'real' one. Dealings mostly take place over the telephone. There are markets in commodities such as gold, oil, and soya beans and, of course, there is a market in government bonds and company shares – the stockmarket.

DIFFERENT WAYS TO BUY FOOD

People with money always try to invest it where it can earn the best return – which often depends on how long they are prepared to invest their money. The more money you have to save or lend – the higher the return. The longer you are prepared to save or lend your money – the higher the return. The more risk you are prepared to take – the higher the return, if all goes well!

INTEREST RATES . . . THE RISE . . .

There are different rates of interest for borrowing, lending, and saving. These interest rates, just like any other sort of price, can be high or low depending on supply and demand. No money market is completely independent of another – and all money markets are affected by interest rates.

If interest rates rise, the cost of borrowing money goes up and so does the amount of return to lenders and savers. This is good for people with money and bad for people without it.

People with money immediately try to make the most of the increased returns offered by the higher interest rates. People from other countries will also invest – raising the value of the national currency and affecting international exchange rates.

People without their own money, or people who are paying a higher price for borrowing money that does not belong to them, have less to spend on other things. This reduction in spending power affects small traders and shopkeepers who may also be paying the higher costs of borrowing. Small companies may have to lay off workers and before you know it, there can be a recession.

. . . AND FALL!

If on the other hand interest rates fall, then there is more money in the borrowers' pockets, they have more to spend and the economy tends to grow.

In such times, the people with money become more choosy about where they invest because they always want to get the biggest possible return for their money.

They will switch their money from saving and lending to buying shares in companies that look like making big profits because they are producing the goods that people seem to want to spend their money on.

It is just like a merry-go-round where the borrowers pay to sit on a horse that goes up and down but never catches the one in front. However, the people who own and work the merry-go-round can go from horse to horse collecting more and more money. They can also decide how long the ride should be according to how many people are queuing up for it. High or low interest rates are like long or short rides.

"I GAINED ON THE SWINGS, Y'KNOW!"

4

THE PUBLIC SECTOR

'PULLING THE WOOL . . .'

To really understand the old saying 'to pull the wool over someone's eyes' you have to imagine what a sheep feels like when it is being sheared. If a sheep doesn't want to be fleeced it wriggles about, so, to calm it down, the shepherd pulls 'the wool' over its eyes in order to temporarily blind the creature to what is going on.

In the jingle jangle jungle of money jargon there is a great deal of mind-boggling mumbo-jumbo that does a similar job; 'a part-convertible subordinated index-linked loan stock with warrants attached' is but an example. Even the experts refer to this sort of gobbledegook as 'funny money'.

Some experts go further and admit that politicians, economists and other professionals in the financial world use such language in order to stop the ordinary person from understanding how money actually works – simply because if everybody knew, then no one would think *they* were very clever!

Whether this is true or not, the fact remains that not only do the experts disguise the essence of what they are up to with strange words, they also frequently use only the initial letters of these words – obscuring what they are talking about even more.

COINING A PHRASE

Because so many of us understand so little about the verbally complex and often totally abstract concepts thrown up by the various disciplines of modern economics, politicians have little or no choice other than to use metaphors in order to get some sort of meaning across.

A metaphor is supposed to help us understand and experience one kind of thing in terms of another.

But, politicians have not necessarily had any training in the basics of economics either – and so we find ourselves being urged to *fight* inflation, to *cure* unemployment, and to look for the *green shoots* of recovery while someone else attempts to *kick-start* the economy!

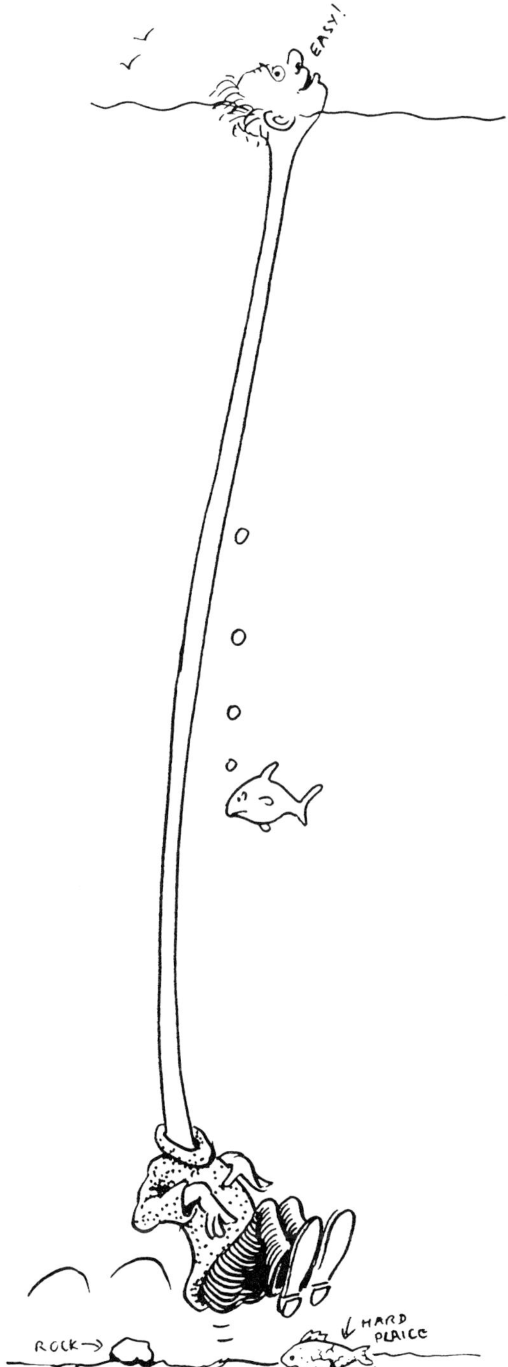

BOUNCING ALONG THE BOTTOM WHILE
KEEPING ONE'S HEAD ABOVE WATER

WHERE THE GOVERNMENT MONEY GOES . . .

The public sector is what politicians and economists have chosen to call central government, local authorities, what's left of the publicly-owned nationalized industries – such as the Post Office and the London Underground – and other public authorities, such as the Health and Safety Executive. It plays a very important part in the British economy, being responsible for a lot of spending and production.

The government spends, or redistributes, about 40% of the national income – all the money we earn from what we all do – and roughly half of this spending is on transfer payments (pensions, unemployment, and child benefits), so-called because they switch spending power from one group of people to another.

The rest is spent on goods and services such as education, medical care, and defence. Even local authorities like a District Council are huge organizations. A medium-sized city will spend several hundred million pounds a year and employ thousands of staff.

"NOW. THIS MONEY COMES FROM EVERYBODY'S TAXES"

. . .AND WHERE IT COMES FROM

Today, most of the nationalized industries – businesses run on behalf of the taxpayers – British Telecom, Gas, Electricity, Water, Oil, Steel, etc; have been sold off to the private sector, or privatized, and no longer provide income, or losses, for the government.

How to 'raise' or get money, and how to spend it – income against expenditure – is called Fiscal or Treasury policy. Like any other business, a government has to pay its bills and when it does not have enough income – which mainly comes from taxes and National Insurance contributions – it has to either cut spending or borrow money in order to balance its books. Raising taxes and cutting public spending on things like National Health and Education, has always been unpopular!

GOVERNMENT BORROWING

Government borrowing is called the Public Sector Borrowing Requirement – or PSBR.

When a government has to borrow money it is always accused of being inefficient so it is much better to announce that you intend to 'increase the PSBR' rather than to admit, more openly, that you need to borrow money!

The government borrows money by issuing various forms of bond. A bond is an IOU, and the terms of the contract between the lender and the borrower are set out on a 'certificate'. This is roughly how it works:

'Lend me some money, let's say £100 – and I'll guarantee to pay it back in 5 years (a short bond), or 10 years (a medium bond), or 15 years (a long bond). I'll also pay you interest every 6 months at a rate of – well, what have I got to offer to make it worth your while? (*haggle, haggle . . .*) OK 10% it is, you drive a hard bargain! Here's a bit of paper that shows everything we've agreed.'

GENTLEMEN PREFER BONDS

The borrower has sold his bond for money and can now go and spend it.

A large number of bonds issued by a borrower used to be called a stock and since most investors buy in multiples of £100 bonds, today they are called stocks.

So a stock is a bond, a bond is an IOU, and an IOU is a certificate. These certificates can be bought and sold like anything else and all things that can be traded on a stock exchange are called securities.

A SENSE OF 'GILT'

'Gilts', a nickname for gilt-edged securities, are government stocks. These stocks are certificates issued by the Bank of England – the central bank of the UK – on behalf of the government Treasury. ('Gilt-edged', some say, because they were once edged with gold – but others say they never were and the name is supposed to have come from the fact that the government guarantees the interest rate as well as repaying the original capital on a specified date! Ho hum. . . .)

So Gilts provide the government with long-term finance – or borrowed money at interest – which they in turn spend on 'our' behalf along with the money raised from all the various forms of taxation.

'ALL THAT GLITTERS . . .'

Meanwhile, speculators are buying and selling these IOUs like crazy! If the economy is weak, the demand for borrowing in the private sector will increase, often forcing the government to put up base interest rates – the *lowest* price of borrowing money – in order to 'strengthen' the pound and attract foreign investors. More about that later!

When interest rates go up, the value of fixed-interest Gilts goes down – and vice versa. So the turnover – or sales – in these government stocks switching from one holder to another can be tremendous as investors frantically try and guess which way the economy is going to turn – up or down.

In 1986, the total turnover of gilt-edged stocks was £424 billion whereas the total value of all stocks listed – short, medium, and long – was only £134 billion. The enormous difference between the turnover and the value reflects the amount of buying and selling and the returns made.

In the same year, new issues totalled £14 billion and all the government got was £7 billion. (New issues are often just to replace stocks that have been redeemed – or paid back!)

While the government still has some control over the money supply – setting interest rates via the Bank of England and other monetary policies – it is becoming increasingly clear that no government can actually control a modern capitalist economy.

CONTROLLING THE 'MONSTER'!

Anatomy shows us how the human body is made up of organs, intestines, skeletal structure, muscles and blood vessels and how they all interact.

An economy, when it is similarly opened up and pulled apart, shows us the way a government, banks, money markets, industries, and individual people pay for themselves and each other, how the money flows between them, and how they create new things and replace what gets used up.

What many radical – and often well-intentioned – economic policy-makers seem to do is to follow in the footsteps of Baron von Frankenstein. Obsessed with their own theories and vision, they attempt to reassemble the perfect economy and give it life.

When the inevitable monster rises from the slab and the villagers are up in arms, all they can do is look around for an Igor to blame!

If the public sector cannot control the economy then how can it control the private sector? Huge profits are there to be taken, simply by moving money around from one investment to another – and making money out of money. Is the ultimate power once again shifting away from those who merely control the money supply, to those who create it?

Who is in charge? Our elected leaders, or those who run multinational corporations or similar monopolies? Is democracy about millions of voters – or thousands of speculators and shareholders looking for increased profits?

Meanwhile – having to keep face with the electorate – having to be as good as the private sector but not being paid as much – to the poor politician and humble civil servant, it must look as if controlling the money supply has lost some of its charm!

MONETARY POLICIES

Devalue money – prices go up

Make money more valuable – prices go down

High Interest Rates make money more valuable

Low Interest Rates make money less valuable

High Interest Rates encourage saving – not spending

Low Interest Rates encourage borrowing – AND spending

Not spending means recession

Spending means growth

What would YOU do?

5

THE PRIVATE SECTOR

DIVIDED WE STAND

Like the bishops and kings of old, modern governments increasingly find themselves playing second fiddle to the all-important market – where producers and consumers come together and where prices are set and regulated by supply and demand.

Money – and human nature – is at the heart of everything. All businesses need money in order to finance the expansion of their means of production and the consumer also needs it to buy more and more of the things they produce.

Industrial nations like Britain and her EC partners, the USA and Japan, all make steel, motor cars, chemicals, and many other commodities on a very large scale.

This means having big corporations – the grouping together of many smaller businesses and companies – which in turn, because of their sheer size, employ vast numbers of people who understandably also group together – in trade unions.

From their united position of strength, the unions can undertake wage-bargaining, negotiate favourable conditions, and otherwise protect the interests of their members in the labour market.

There are of course smaller businesses in the private sector – like farming, specialist shops, and other consumer services – which work better on a small scale.

MARKET FORCES

NO COMPETITION

But like money, the market is becoming more and more of an idea than a reality. The undeniable trend in the private sector is for bigger and bigger businesses, the ruthless elimination of competition and consequently, no effective market regulation of prices.

The corner shop is being replaced by the drive-in supermarkets, the small builder is being squeezed by the property developers, there are fast-food franchises and shopping malls in every town with the same name retail outlets as everywhere else – all controlled by a few really big organizations each financed by selling part-ownership to thousands of shareholders.

Whenever the market fails to regulate prices it is usually because demand for a certain commodity is high and there is no real competition among suppliers.

WHAT CAN HAPPEN

When OPEC – the Organization of Petroleum Exporting Countries – got together and decided to raise their prices by 66% in October 1973 and a further 100% in January 1974, no one could stop them and governments worldwide had to intervene.

Up until then, oil prices had been arguably cheap and many economies were enjoying a period of rapid growth. This 'boom' came to a very abrupt end.

In Britain, the government formed the Social Contract with the trade unions to freeze wage demands and match the fall in the national income caused by the oil price rise.

Public sector borrowing was reduced and so was the growth rate in the money supply. This led to cuts in public spending and to devaluing the pound.

Drastic measures, but they were largely successful. By 1977, inflation fell, the balance of payments increased, and sterling appreciated.

However, by 1979, faith in the market returned. The private sector was itching to make more profits again, nobody wanted prices and incomes controls. Wages rose, output rose, consumer spending rose, but so did inflation and unemployment!

6

A HOUSE OF CARDS

EVERYONE has heard of inflation and unemployment – they are almost always in the news – probably because politicians and economists don't *really* know what to do about either of them! Let's take inflation first.

THE BALLOON GOES UP!

Inflation is steadily rising prices – not just some going up and others going down, but all or most going up together. This includes wages and salaries because they are the prices people put on their skills and their labour. But why does this happen?

Let's go back to the idea of money. Money is a measure of the value of things we want. In the old days, people who wanted to sell and people who wanted to buy came together in the market. The market was a very good way of working out prices – because of supply and demand and competition. Fair prices were almost guaranteed.

If you wanted to buy some fruit, you could look around until you found the person selling the best fruit at the best price. It was the same with eggs, milk, pots, pans, weapons, clothes, and everything else that people could want. All important needs were supplied. Things in short supply cost more – things that were plentiful cost less, but inflation as we know it today – ALL prices going up together – was almost impossible.

Inflation could only happen then if there was an increase in the supply of the basic money. After the discovery of the Americas, the mines of Mexico and Peru poured a large quantity of precious metals, mostly silver, into Europe. (It came from Indian labour in the mines, not from the accumulated treasure of the Aztecs and the Incas.) In consequence, all prices were very high, because the value of the 'plentiful' money was low.

WHAT! MORE GOLD!

'BATTERIES NOT INCLUDED'

Nowadays, the things we want are marketed in a much more aggressive way and many different forces affect the prices we have to pay. If you wanted to buy the very latest video game you would have to pay the price the shop was asking, because the makers of the game and the shopkeepers will have agreed, AND advertised, a recommended retail price.

This control of prices is quite recent. Since big businesses started buying up other businesses and forming themselves into big corporations, they soon found they could charge more or less what they liked for the things they produced.

Most businesses are employers, buyers, sellers, and money makers. Somebody makes something, buys something, or does something, and sells it to someone else for money. 'Sales' means money coming in, 'costs' means money going out, 'profit' or 'loss' means the difference between sales and costs. The bigger the business, the more important it is to a country's economy.

When a big business owns the factories where your favourite video game is made, AND the chain of shops that sell it, you can see how easy it is for them to sell it at a high price and make a large profit – because they have no competition. This is called a monopoly.

" SO, WHY IS THERE ONLY ONE MONOPOLIES COMMISSION ?"

UP, UP, AND AWAY!

When enough prices start to rise in this way, people soon start to demand higher wages – the price *they* charge for what they do.

The big corporations can afford to meet *their* workers' demands, not only because of their big profits, but also because they can control their prices. They can pay their workers more, put up their prices – thus passing on the cost to the consumer – and still make the same profit.

Many workers belong to trade unions, organizations that represent their interests, but not everybody in a trade union works for a big corporation. When a trade union successfully demands a pay rise, all the other members are entitled to it. Very often smaller businesses employing union members cannot pay these increased costs. They either go out of business, or reduce the number of people working for them in order to cut costs. Either way, this means a lot of people lose their jobs – in other words, causing unemployment.

WHO'S TO BLAME?

Some small businesses, operating on borrowed money, have to borrow *more* money – if they are to do the same amount of business at the higher prices – just to keep going. So the banks, along with the extra spending power of those with higher wages, also increase the money supply by lending more money – this also adds to the inflation.

So, banks shove up prices, wage demands shove up prices, and large corporations pass the higher costs on to the public because they can control their prices in the market AND make the same margin of profit. This upward wage/price spiral is the central cause of present-day inflation – the steady rise of ALL prices.

THE SAFEST WAY TO DOUBLE YOUR MONEY

What can anyone do about it? Very little it would seem. Trying to control wage rises and prices is unpopular with nearly everyone because it stops the great social desire for higher consumption. All of us want more of the good things in life.

Even so, most people would agree that it is a sad fact of life that today, the only way of reducing inflation seems to be at the cost of very high levels of unemployment – throwing a great many people out of work in order to keep everything else going.

THIS MEANS YOU!

The vast majority of people have never owned the means of creating wealth. For centuries they have had to sell their labour and skills in return for wages – simply in order to buy the things they need.

They have no land – nowhere to build, nowhere to grow their own food – they can only seek employment from those who control the means of production. All these people have to have money – simply to be able to survive within the laws of property ownership and let's face it, such laws were hardly drawn up with *their* interests in mind!

Remember, because it can be bought and sold, human labour is also a commodity and if there is no demand for what you can do – you can become unemployed.

"MONEY TALKS ALRIGHT!"

IT'S ONLY HUMAN NATURE

The word recession has been borrowed by politicians and economists – it means: 'the action of receding; withdrawal, retirement, or departing.' It may be safe to suppose that in economic terms it generally means that things are bad, but when politicians says we are 'bouncing along the bottom of a recession', anyone can be excused for not knowing what they are talking about!

However, it is well known that politicians and economists often disagree about what causes what and who is to blame for things going wrong. In 1936, John Maynard Keynes wrote a book called *The General Theory of Employment, Interest, and Money*. Many experts call him a 'bighead' and a 'self-publicist' but grudgingly admit he is mostly right.

Keynes assumed the possibility that natural economic processes – like recessions and booms – could be cumulative (added to) rather than compensatory (counterbalancing). That is to say, once an economy started moving in a different way (up or down, forward or back, receding or advancing – take your pick!), then that *movement* would get stronger, not weaker, according to how people reacted.

This, he reckoned, was because of human nature. As consumers, savers, and producers we all tend to be short-sighted and selfish as well as the victims of greed – our own or someone else's. We are constantly surprised when our plans don't work out and disappointed when we don't get what we want.

MISERABLE MISERS!

How much we buy or generally use up as consumers depends upon how much money we have in our pockets – if we're lucky enough to have some to spare, we might want to save it. If enough people decide to become savers – even though there may be plenty of things in the shops they could easily buy – this can slow down the economy and confuse the producers. They tend to be cautious and judge future demand, or how much they should produce, on how much people are spending now.

People save money – and we are often told that this is a good thing to do – so that they can earn interest from the bank or building society that looks after their deposits. They can watch their money grow.

The producers do not see that some people might be saving simply to be able to buy more of their product at a later date, when they feel they have enough money put by.

When, and if, this sudden demand comes along, the producers are frequently unprepared – the things they sell are in short supply – forcing prices up and probably cancelling out any interest the savers might have earned. Even worse, when they first noticed that people were saving and not spending, the producers may have laid off workers in order to cut costs! Thanks to human nature, just about everybody loses.

MOTHER HUBBARD'S CUPBOARD

Naturally, how much we consume also depends on how little we have in our pockets. If nobody bought *anything* – apart from the bare necessities of life – it could turn a minor recession into a full economic depression. (Another borrowed word meaning: 'A lowering in quality, vigour, or amount; the state of being lowered' – if a recession is bad, a depression is terrible!)

A depression happens when a great many people suddenly find themselves out work. Through no fault of their own, they are forced to live on a reduced income. They immediately have to stop spending at the rate they could when they earned a wage or salary. But they still have to pay their bills – and while they may get some money from the government, it is certainly not enough to keep them at the same standard of living that they were once used to.

They can no longer afford bikes for birthdays, cars, holidays, or even fashionable clothes. They may even have to lose the house they were buying on a mortgage.

A mortgage is just another way of borrowing money – if for some reason you can't pay the money back, the lender can take your house or property instead of the money.

In a depression, just about everybody suffers. Banks lose to businesses that collapse owing them money, shops close owing to lack of customers, investors have no confidence in new businesses, and those still in work are generally taxed higher so that governments can 'pay' the unemployed.

Unemployment is very expensive for a government – it is curious that while so many people are paid to do nothing, those still in work have to work harder to keep up productivity!

But the hardships endured by those who can still earn a living are nothing compared to the misery of being unemployed. The Great Depression took place in the 1930s and today, the arguments still go on about how to get a country out of recession. Some talk of getting inflation down, others talk of 'consumer confidence', 'sustainable growth' and 'wealth creation', but what they are all hoping for is some kind of boom to happen.

"ONLY THE PRICE HAS SUFFERED FROM SUBSIDENCE...."

THE KLONDIKE FACTOR

If anyone knew how to create a continuous boom, they would have done it a long time ago. A boom is rather like a 'Gold Rush' – suddenly something valuable and in short supply becomes available. Towns and businesses spring up all around the area where 'gold' has been discovered – people get rich and start spending their money. For a while it lasts, but then the 'gold' runs out.

In the mid-1980s in Britain, home ownership boomed and property prices soared. People were encouraged to borrow money against the new high value of their homes and spend it on luxuries they had always dreamed of. But like the 'gold', and the real sixteenth-century silver from Mexico and Peru, the borrowed money, or credit, only increased the money supply and the value of money went down just as all prices steadily went up – resulting in inflation and unemployment and the recession of the late 1980s and the early 90s.

Who knows when the next boom: 'A start of commercial activity; a rush of activity in business or speculation' – will happen?

Meanwhile, money-making, industry, and consumerism have grown so much that they are now threatening the very environmental resources of the planet that all living creatures depend on for their basic survival. This is why politicians and economists keep talking about 'sustainable growth'. It is a very complex problem indeed.

How long can the planet supply all the raw materials we turn into things we consume? How long can the environment put up with all the pollution pumped out by the industrialized nations? Why do the 'developing' countries want to expand in the same way?

NO MORE MISTER NICE GAIA!

I'M SURE THERE
A SIMPLE ANS
SOMEBODY HELP!
DONT
TOLD YOU SO
WHERES THE LIGHT?
OK, WHAT'S HAPPENED?
THANKS

GLOOM AND DOOM

The whole world seems to believe in economic growth but is there enough to go round? Is the basic greed of making money shaking the very table that supports the 'house of cards'? Wow! Read on . . .

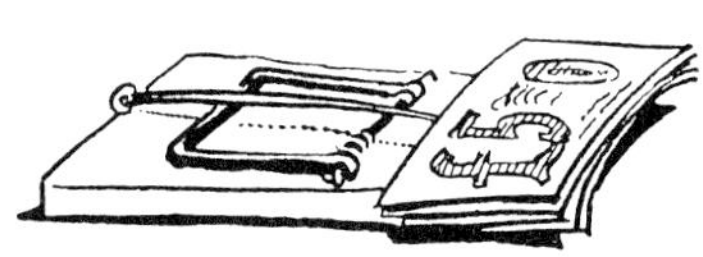

7

STOCKS AND SHARES

'TWO'S COMPANY . . .'

In order to understand what stocks and shares are, it is helpful to know what a company is. A company is a business that is owned by more than one person and it has special rights and protection by law – in return for obeying certain rules.

Once a business has legally become a company, the people who own it are no longer *personally* responsible for any debts, complaints, or claims against it. If the business goes bust – owing money to others – the owners only lose what they invested – or put into it.

The creditors – people who are owed money by the company – cannot take away the owners' personal possessions in place of payment by the company, they can only share what is left of the liquidated assets – the money got from selling off whatever belonged to the company.

This protection is called limited liability – without it, many businesses would not get started. There are many reasons why a business can fail and it is not always the fault of the people who run it. For the same reasons, people should not invest any more money than they can afford to lose!

PROS AND CONS

More often than not, the creditors get less than they are owed. This may not seem fair, but it would be equally unfair if people lost their homes and all their possessions because of something they could do nothing about.

On the other hand, the rules for companies are very strict and the responsibilities clearly defined. You cannot 'close' your company without warning and you must publish information about how much money your business has.

These rules help businesses to trade with each other. Companies will let other companies buy much larger amounts of goods and let them pay much later than an individual or 'non-company' small business.

Most businesses want to become companies because banks are company businesses too, and *they* would rather deal with and lend money to other companies – rather than to individuals or small partnerships.

All businesses need money to get started and borrowing from a bank is the usual way of going about it. This starting-up money is called capital – because it is at the head or the first thing you need when you go into business.

HOW IT ALL BEGAN

But if you own a company, you can also raise capital from selling parts of it – *instead* of borrowing from a bank. A part – or a share of the ownership – of the company can be sold to others in return for cash.

The business of buying and selling shares, as we know it, only began about 300 years ago when European merchants – rather like Shakespeare's Antonio in Venice – wanted to expand their trade with the newly-discovered countries in Africa, America, and the Far East.

They knew that big profits could be made by simply going and getting the silks, spices, tobacco, and ivory, because of the high demand for them at home.

But buying a seaworthy ship, feeding a crew, and taking enough gold and goods to exchange was very expensive. So, to finance the voyage, the merchants needed to raise a lot of money. If the banks wouldn't lend them enough – shipping was, and still is, a risky business – they could raise *more* capital from investors, usually friends or aquaintances.

Investors would lend money in return for bond certificates – pieces of paper saying how much they had put in, what interest they would get, and even a date when they would be paid back. These IOUs became known as stock.

HOW IT DEVELOPED

In the late seventeenth century, all sorts of companies were formed to raise capital for business ventures by issuing 'certificates' in return for money. A company would offer a large number, or stock of these certificates at a single time and perhaps hundreds of people would buy them.

That way, a much larger number of people could invest – or put in money – than one or two banks, who were always worried about taking too much risk on their own. Even today, these bits of paper – or certificates – issued by companies *and* governments alike – are still referred to as stocks. This is also how the place where they are bought and sold became known as the stock exchange.

It was soon discovered however, that it was much better to sell shares – or part-ownership – in the company rather than repay stocks in full for one particular venture.

When the voyage was over and the profit made, each shareholder got a *small* part of the profit – the dividend – in proportion to the size of their individual share. The rest of the profit would be kept by the company to help pay off the bankers and finance the next voyage.

HOW IT IS TODAY

Nowadays, once a company is formed, a board of directors is appointed – usually shareholders themselves – to decide future policy and report to any other shareholders, while the management concerns itself with the day-to-day running of the business.

Ordinary or A shareholders can come together and vote on company policy at an Annual General Meeting, or at special extraordinary meetings if a merger or a takeover is in the offing.

ANNUAL GENERAL MEETING.

If even more capital is needed to finance expansion or the takeover of another company, special issues of B or non-voting shares can be floated on the stockexchange.

EXTRAORDINARY GENERAL MEETING

8

CORPORATIONS AND MULTINATIONALS

GETTING 'QUOTED' OR 'FLOATED'

If there are advantages in turning a business into a company, then the potential benefits from gathering lots of companies into a corporation are truly staggering.

But first a company must be big enough to be listed on a stock exchange. Most businesses are content to remain as private companies – their shares may be owned by a family or a few friends – but when a company decides to go public all sorts of things can happen.

RUNNERS AND RIDERS

No one really knows what the shares of a private company are worth, because they are not for sale to the public – or to put it more plainly, no one can *gamble* on them. Public – or listed companies are just like horses in a race – people can bet on them in the hope that they might win and make *more* money for them than the amount they initially invested – in other words, a return.

Because anyone can buy shares in them, big public corporations and multinationals – hundreds of big and small international businesses grouped together – can be jointly owned by thousands of people all over the world.

"THERE, LOOK, THAT'S MY OLD COMPANY"

They are the favourites in the horse race not least because they employ the best jockeys – professional management teams – highly skilled in the psychology of marketing, labour relations, cost-cutting, creative accounting, and totally dedicated to making a profit for their shareholders.

THE FAVOURITE IN THE RACE

John Kenneth Galbraith – a rare economist with a sense of fun – calls these managers the 'technostructure'.

UNDER STARTER'S ORDERS

So, apart from raising extra cash from selling new shares to the public, there are at least two other reasons why companies 'go for a listing' – or 'come to the market', 'go public', 'seek a quotation' or a 'flotation' (they all mean the same thing) – one is to find out the *true* value of the existing shares in the market – for the benefit of the existing shareholders – and the second is to join the big league with its vast potential for profits and growth, power and influence.

First of all, a company must put together a report showing how well it has done over the past few years, how much its assets – property and equipment – are worth, and what profits it expects to make in the future.

Then the report is taken to a special banker and stockbroker who will handle the sale of the company shares – with all the necessary paperwork – and generally give advice.

Because no one really knows what the shares are worth, the company, the banker, and the broker will have to sit down and guess what the right price is.

If they guess too low, the company and the existing share-holders won't get as much cash as they could have got.

If they guess too high, nobody will want to buy the shares.

THEY'RE OFF!

However, once a company has gone public it can really begin to grow. Its shares can be bought and sold on the stock exchange and if it is run wisely and makes lots of profits, the value of the shares will increase and soon it will have enough money to make a bid – or try to buy another company.

TAKEOVERS AND MERGERS

When a company bids for another company – perhaps a rival or competitor in a similar business – the board of directors of the target company may advise their shareholders either to agree or to defend or contest the bid, but it is the shareholders who have the last word – by voting.

If everyone agrees to sell, it is called a merger, but if they do not want to be 'bought out' – and the bidding company gains control of enough shares – it is called a takeover.

In order to gain control of the other business, the bidding company has to be able to buy at least 50.1 per cent of the shares of that company.

Some shareholders may wish to sell, others may not, and there are several ways of persuading – but let's not go into them except to say that they all involve making money or a return!

9

THE STOCK EXCHANGE

The modern Stock Exchange is a far cry from the cosy little coffee shops in London – or under the tree in New York – where the first capitalists met to do business. Nowadays, all over the world there are stock exchanges linked by telephones, computers, and even satellites in space.

Like any other money market, the stock exchanges are in business to make more money out of existing money – but remember that ALL businesses – especially those that make the things we like to consume – need money to get started.

The more money a stock exchange can make generally means that there is more money to invest in other profit-making enterprises – and so creating wealth for an economy as a whole.

Of course sometimes things can go wrong, but ever since stocks and shares have been bought and sold in order to raise capital, businesses and economies have visibly continued to grow – through the science and technology of the industrial revolution and on and on – into the vast and ever-expanding world trade and profit-making we know today.

THE BROKERS

How a modern stock exchange works is basically the same as the old coffee shops – only much, much bigger and more varied. Until recently, only official members of the stock exchange, and their employees, were allowed to work there.

If an ordinary member of the public wishes to buy or sell shares in a company, he or she must go to a broker – someone who brings buyers and sellers together. Suppose you owned 1,000 shares in a company that was just starting and you bought the shares for £1 each. After a while, the company is successful and you would like to sell some of your shares.

You find a broker who says he knows someone who is willing to pay £2 per share – because the company is profitable and has grown. You could then decide to sell 500 shares to the new buyer for £1,000 – and use that money to invest in something else that might grow in the same way.

Not only has your original investment doubled, but the remaining shares you own in the company could also be worth even more if the company continues to grow.

Of course if the company does badly for some reason, then your shares would be worth less and a stockbroker might have a hard time persuading someone else to buy them off you!

The stockbroker charges a fee called a commission – usually a small percentage of the value of the deal – for acting as a go-between. He may charge more if he gives you advice on what to buy or sell.

But just as investors are not allowed to deal directly with each other – in order to prevent secret buying and selling above or below the market price of a share – so too, the brokers are not allowed to deal between themselves, for the same reason. They have to go to other members of the stock exchange called market-makers.

THE MARKET-MAKERS

Market-makers buy and sell shares and in doing so, set a price for those shares. They usually give two prices for a company's share. A higher price when they sell and a lower price when they buy. The difference, called the spread, is what they keep as payment for their work.

It is a highly skilled and risky business because – share prices can go *down* as well as up – and market-makers have to compete with other market-makers and often deal in the same company shares. It's not that easy being 'something in the city'.

MARKET 'MOODS'

Economies are so inextricably linked to human nature that it is virtually impossible to predict what will happen next with any certainty. Sometimes a mood of gloom can affect the money markets and prices will begin to fall, at other times a feeling of hope can make prices rise.

These moods are when the bears and bulls are said to be on the loose. A bear is anyone who thinks share prices are going to fall for one reason or another and sells his or her shares *before* they do. If share prices in general start falling, then it is called a bear market.

BULLS AND BEARS

A bull does just the opposite – he or she believes share prices are going to go up and starts buying before they do. When prices start to rise all across the market as a consequence – it is called a bull market.

WHAT CAN HAPPEN

Even though many modern stock exchanges no longer operate from just one building with a trading floor – rumours about this and that still fly about.

Since deregulation, brokers, market-makers, and banks have combined as complete businesses themselves and many occupy their own new office blocks, but they are all still in constant touch with competitors and other markets all around the world by telephone, computer, and satellite.

Now gossip can whizz right across the globe in a matter of seconds. But is this progress?

In 1987, the world stock market crash began in New York where people were worried about the American economy. Share prices worldwide were at an all-time high, so some investors figured that they must be about to go down and switched from equity – shares in companies – to fixed-interest stocks and bonds.

This trickle of selling showed up so quickly on the modern computer and telecommunication systems that almost immediately, more and more brokers started frantically selling off vast numbers of shares in order to protect their clients.

This made Tokyo, where they were just starting the day's business, also sell huge amounts of shares. Later in London, when they too started business, they did the same thing and when New York reopened for business – there was panic! Followed by more frenzied selling in Tokyo, and again in London. Very soon, markets across the world – Germany, France, Canada, Australia, Hong Kong – all went crashing down with them.

BLACK MONDAY

WHY THE CHANGE?

What was wrong with the old system? Once again, money is at the centre of it all. Before 1986, market-makers were known as jobbers.

During fixed trading hours, they bought and sold shares hoping to make a profit on the spread between their buying and selling price. The speed of the transactions also depended on how quickly a jobber could obtain cash.

Jobbers were only allowed to deal with each other and brokers, who in turn were the only ones who could act as agents for the public – charging them a commission for dealing with the jobbers on their behalf.

Because the old stock exchange had imposed a scale of fixed commissions for the brokers, and because the cost of the jobbers' services was met by the investor, the government decided that enough was enough and that these outdated methods were inefficient, restrictive, and expensive.

'BIG BANGS' AND LITTLE BRAINS

The New York Stock Exchange had abandoned fixed commissions in 1975 in favour of negotiated commissions and British brokers realized their incomes would be greatly reduced unless they too could act as market-makers.

So after much haggling and pushing from the government, the London Stock Exchange finally scrapped the rule against outside ownership of broking and jobbing businesses and became deregulated on October 27th 1986.

Now banks, or any other institution with a lot of cash, can go into partnership with stockbrokers and market-makers. This change became known as the 'Big Bang' – after the latest theory on the creation of the ever-expanding universe!

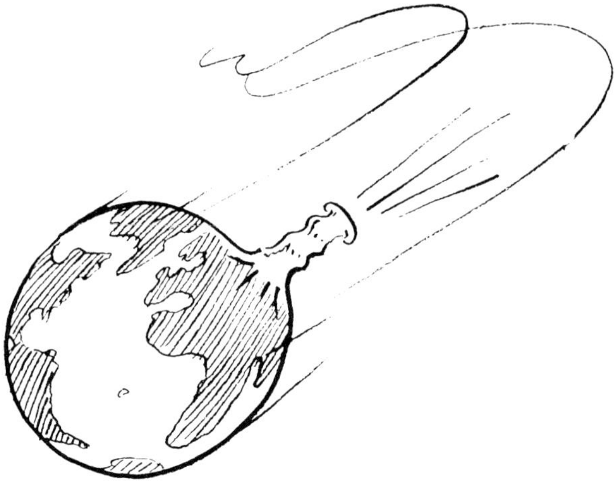

It's rather like the old Abbott and Costello joke: 'Once upon a time, there were two Irishmen – now look how many there are!'

(My sincere apologies to the great Irish people – but I suppose the 'joke' refers just as well to Belgians, Brits, Poles, Norwegians . . . or even Essex Girls!)

10

FOREIGN EXCHANGE RATES

MONEY MAKES THE WORLD GO AROUND

In simple money terms, every country in the world has its 'haves' and 'have nots' and it is worth remembering the old saying that 'a rich man is a poor man with lots of money'.

In today's modern money markets people with money can easily invest in any country where they feel their money can get the *biggest* profit, capital gain, or return.

In every country, money flows around the economy and this is why any sort of money, *currently* being used anywhere, is called a currency.

Up to now, we have looked at money in only simple terms. We know that money is basically an idea, but what is the money supply we hear so much about?

The liquid metaphor occurs everywhere in economics:
liquid assets = cash
near liquid = easily turnable into cash
liquidate = turn into cash
liquidated assets = things sold for cash
liquidation = selling everything for cash
liquidator = someone who sells your things for cash
liquidity = the ability to turn things into cash
liquidity ratio = how much cash a bank thinks it ought to keep on deposit for depositors who might want their money at any time.

Then there is 'floating' a company – or stockmarket 'launches', 'floating charges, exchange rates, and interest rates' – as opposed to fixed ones – getting production 'on stream' . . . zzzzzzzzzzzzzzzzzzzz . . ..NO! Someone throw a bucket of water over them!

THE MONEY SUPPLY

Economists divide money into liquid and non-liquid assets. They find the distinction between liquid and non-liquid hard to make precise because 'liquidity is a matter of degree, assets being more or less liquid, rather than simply liquid or non-liquid'. (Gulp!)

LIQUIDITY IS A MATTER OF DEGREE

In other words, the money supply is equal to cash in the public's hands and deposits in a bank.

Banking either holds deposits as reserves or lends them back to the public. High-powered money – or the monetary base, means the quantity of reserve assets – this is defined as cash and reserves.

THE MONEY TREE

WHAT IS M1, M2, M3, M4, ETC.?

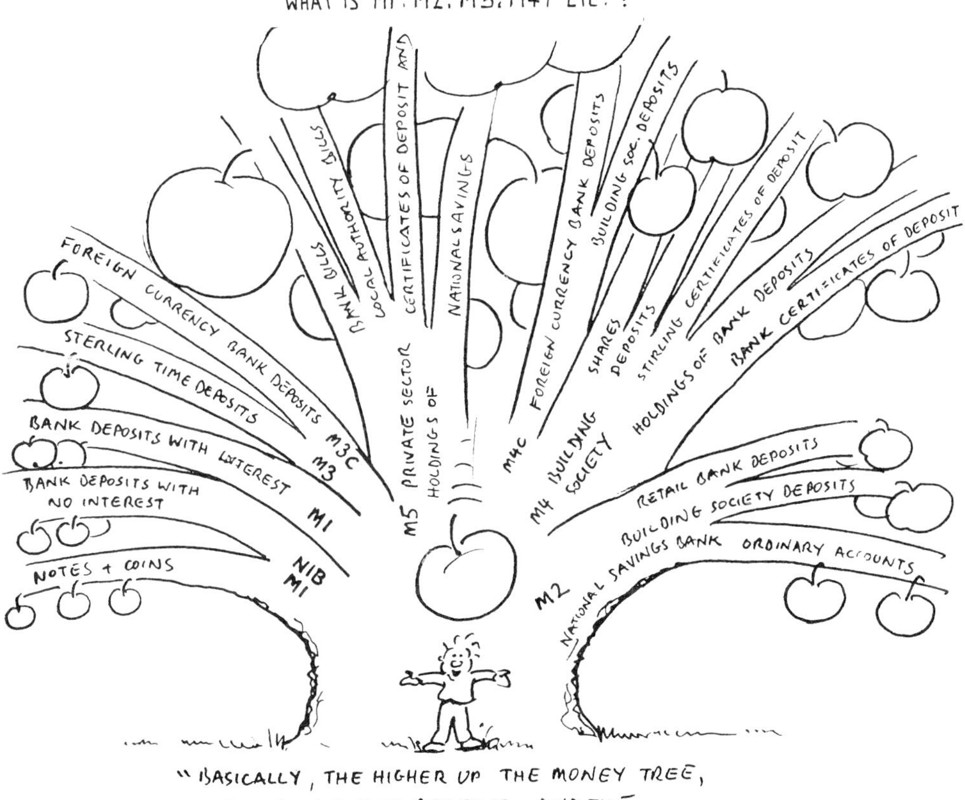

"BASICALLY, THE HIGHER UP THE MONEY TREE, THE HARDER IT IS TO GET TO IT, AND THE BIGGER IT GROWS!"

In the old days when cash meant gold coins and when banks held gold as reserves – the high-powered money would be gold.

Nowadays, banks hold a wide variety of assets as reserves, not simply Bank of England notes and deposits, but also Treasury stocks and bonds, as well as investments in shares in the private sector that can easily be converted back into cash.

The banks have a legally imposed reserve ratio but are also regulated by considerations of risk. If enough depositors suddenly lose confidence in a bank, and all of them want to withdraw their money at the same time, a run on the bank develops and the chances are that the bank would not have enough cash available to go round and it would be forced to close its doors.

ONLY MAKE-BELIEVE

That's why confidence is all-important in the banking world. If EVERYBODY who had money in a bank somewhere wanted to withdraw it, there is no way all the banks could quickly get back all the money they had invested or advanced to borrowers, they would all have to close their doors and the whole monetary system would collapse!

"...OF COURSE YOU CAN HAVE ALL YOUR MONEY, AT ANY TIME YOU WANT IT!"

It is the same in every other country in the world and if another country's banking system offers higher interest rates than your own country, you may be tempted to invest your money there.

All you have to do is change your money into the currency – whatever its name is – your chosen country uses. This is done by buying that currency on the foreign exchange market.

If enough people like you want to buy that currency, its value will rise and – if you were one of the *first* to buy – you will not only gain from the higher interest rates on offer, you will also gain from the rise in the value of the foreign currency you now own.

In other words you could sell your foreign currency for more than you paid for it and add that to the higher return you got from the favourable foreign interest rates.

This is why governments sometimes deliberately raise interest rates – to attract foreign investors and so increase the value of their own money in circulation, or national currency.

They also like to hold foreign currency reserves in their central banks in case the value of their own money should fall. So governments often invest in other currencies from countries with strong economies – like the dollar, the Deutschmark and the yen.

Perhaps this is a good time to remind ourselves that money was – always has been – and still is – an idea. It is something that we – as human beings – have thought up all by ourselves. You don't see other animals or plants queuing up to stick bits of plastic into walls for something they can't eat – no, it's only because enough of us believe it is valuable that money is worth anything to us at all.

" THIS WAY, WE GET TO FLEECE OURSELVES "

So how is one currency valued against another? Yet another idea of course! The measuring of economic growth – or recession, and the belief in those measurements.

TWO WAYS OF MEASURING AN ECONOMY

Gross Domestic Product, or GDP, is not some unspeakably vile cardigan knitted by someone's maiden aunt, it is the declared total value, in current prices, of everything a country produces or sells in the course of a year – including the cost value of all public services – such as transport, electricity, and water.

National Income is similar; it is the declared total annual income of everyone in the country who has made a profit, or earned a wage or salary, from producing and selling their goods, services, skills, or labour.

GDP is more or less the same thing as National Income – but NEITHER shows us what any good housekeeper needs to know – how much money a country *actually* has in the bank!

What's more, GDP can only measure the value of things that have a known price, such as weapons, coal, or shampoo that hasn't been tested on animals.

A nurse looking after someone elderly gets paid a certain amount of money, a parent looking after a sick child does not. Both are performing a similar service but because it is impossible to put a price on the value of their love, only the nurse's wages go into the Gross Domestic Product.

Both National Income and Gross Domestic Product are just the names given to established ways of measuring a country's economic growth or decline – just as there are two ways of using a clinical thermometer. Whichever place you choose to stick it, you can find out what your temperature is – but not necessarily what is wrong with you!

Economic growth is the steady increase in output of all the things we consume, use up, invest in or otherwise produce. For example, instead of eating 2 bags of crisps every day, you eat 3; instead of making 10 cans of fizzy drinks a second, a factory makes 12; and so on . . .

Therefore, to the ordinary person, it is hardly a cause for wild celebration if the GDP goes up OR down! It has no immediate effect on the *real* quality of life. But for a politician, it can be used to show the success, or failure, of an economic policy, and as such it is of little value to the man in the street and we might as well ignore it.

ANOTHER WAY OF MEASURING AN ECONOMY

How a country's stock exchange is doing is considered to be a more *meaningful* sign of health or sickness in an economy. Every stock exchange in the world publishes a share index of one sort or another and these are generally used to measure movement in ordinary share prices.

If share prices go up – the index goes up, if share prices fall – so does the index. All movements are measured in points and if the points are high it means an economy is doing well – and vice versa.

In New York they use the Dow Jones index, in Tokyo the Nikkei Dow, in Hong Kong the Hang Seng – to name but a few. In Britain the most widely-reported share index is the Financial Times Stock Exchange 100-Share Index, the FT-SE or 'Footsie' (our financial people can be SO cute!).

Stock exchanges turn over and make enormous sums of money and when it shows up in GDP or National Income it is referred to as invisible earnings and becomes part of a nation's capital account – which shows the flow of capital funds, loans, investments, etc. into and out of that country.

. . .YET ANOTHER WAY . . .

Then there is the balance of payments in the current account. This measures the difference between the value of imports and exports of any country. When there is a surplus it means a country is exporting – or selling – more of what it does, or makes, than importing.

When there is a deficit, a country is importing – or buying more stuff from abroad – than it exports.

If a country has a current account balance of payments surplus then it obviously has a successful economy – low inflation, low unemployment – and that country's currency will be strong and rising in value and therefore tempting to foreign investors.

All these methods of measuring can signal the strength or weakness of a country's economy, but the daily share index probably has the most affect on the value of international currencies in the foreign exchange money markets.

. . .AND ONE MORE!

The other theory of how to value different currencies relies on measuring the purchasing power of one or more currencies against another. This involves measuring retail prices – via the retail price index – the cost of goods in shops, etc. – and measuring inflation over a one year period.

The only problem is deciding on where to start measuring the 12 month period. What is a typical year? Anyway, it would seem that the people who speculate in the Forex market – or foreign exchange markets – aren't really bothered about accurate valuations even if they were reliable.

The global currency market is 32 times larger than world trade flows – there was a global turnover of 650 billion US dollars a day in April 1989. Some people are obviously making a lot of money out of foreign exchange rates!

What all this frenzied buying and selling is doing to the global money supply – and consequently the speculators own national economies – doesn't bear thinking about.

Sadly, whatever they're doing doesn't seem to worry them too much. Others, like manufacturers, exporters and suppliers of raw materials, would like to see the ERM – Exchange Rate Mechanism – bring the EC currencies closer to EMU – European Monetary Union – and start using the ECU – European Currency Unit – as soon as possible.

A single currency would benefit manufacturers and exporters, stabilise trade and prices, and hopefully reduce unemployment.

But who can tell? Whichever way you slice the economy you will find conflicting interests. So what of the future? Was Thomas Hobbes right when he said we needed a really strong authority to control the innate hostility of self-interest?

Or shall we find the Utopian common wealth that Thomas More so wishfully described?

Who knows? Even Adam Smith warned against monopolies ruining the market's natural ability to regulate prices through competition – how would he deal with the foreign currency speculators, multinationals, and big corporations we have today?

11

CRYSTAL BALLS

WORLD MARKETS

'Globalization' became a buzz-word in financial circles during the 1980s. The deregulation of the money markets, the improved computer and telecommunications technology, together with the scrapping of fixed exchange rates, suddenly allowed investors, for the very first time, to begin worldwide trading in both currencies and bonds.

World trade is nothing new – markets in raw materials, or primary commodities, have been international for as long as anyone can remember – but the more recent development of international and multinational corporations have so increased the growth of trade in goods and services on a global scale, that they, in a sense, have opened the door to international trading in just about everything.

Apart from anything else, the shop window in the high street can tell you that prices can go down as well as up and ALL financial investments involve an element of risk. There is no such thing as a safe bet or a certainty and the limitation or the management of risk is a key factor in all money markets.

EVEN MULTINATIONALS CAN LOSE THEIR HEADS...

ACHTUNG! ATTENTION! PERICOLOSO! WARNING!

'Don't put all your eggs in one basket' is a good principle when it comes to investment risk-management.

A stockbroker will operate a portfolio of shares – shares in different companies – and spread the risk for a shareholder. Pension Fund managers will invest in different currencies and bonds in order to safeguard the contributors' money.

But the risks of international trading are much higher than they are at home. It is very possible to mistime when to buy or sell and good planning can often be ruined by sudden movements in foreign currencies.

The world money markets are themselves like financial instruments in a global portfolio.

(Financial instruments are securities or anything else that can be bought and sold on a stock exchange.)

Governments and banks can now invest all around the world in each other – and so spread the risk of something going wrong somewhere, sometime, as well as increasing their chances of making a return.

Multinationals can turn to foreign investors for new equity (shares) capital – the parent company's home capital market may be too small for them!

There are two more good reasons for them to do this. Since they make things, buy things, sell things and employ people in many different countries – they need liquidity or cash in those different currencies to meet their local costs.

Also, by placing shares all around the world, the risk of a takeover is greatly reduced. By having so many shareholders scattered all over the place, rival corporate raiders would find great difficulty in getting to them.

FUTURES AND OPTIONS

'Look before you leap' is another good principle and it is probably this sort of risk-limitation that has led to the extraordinary growth in Futures, Swaps, and Options.

These relatively new financial instruments are called derivatives because they are derived from underlying or non-primary commodities (like frozen orange juice) and financial instruments (like securities).

Primary commodities are raw materials – with little or no processing done to them other than to pack them into agreed units of size, weight, volume or whatever. (Ingots of metal, barrels of oil, bushels of wheat, etc.)

Because primary commodities are so vital to so many underlying commodities – things made from raw materials – and the businesses that process them, their prices can be very high or very low because of good old supply and demand again.

TRADING FUTURES AND OPTIONS

Traditionally, fortunes have been made and lost dealing in raw materials, as a consequence, arriving at the right prices in the commodity markets has remained of vital importance – because they obviously affect the prices of nearly everything else.

A future is a contract between two parties, the seller – who agrees to supply a certain amount of a commodity on a certain date in the future, and a buyer – who agrees to purchase the specified amount at a pre-determined price on the same date.

"...SO LET'S GET THIS RIGHT – YOU WANT TO BUY FUTURES TODAY IN TWO POUNDS OF COURGETTES NEXT THURSDAY...."

The purpose of any market is to discover prices, the cost in money of something in demand to someone who supplies it. Unlike many other markets, with their computers and price indices flashing continuously across the screens, commodity markets still trade in the traditional face-to-face manner known as 'open outcry'.

Bids and offers are shouted out so that they can be heard by everybody. This prevents any cheating or secret price-fixing. Traders stand on the steps of a trading pit, shouting and waving their hands – with their own special buy and sell hand signals – just in case their shouts are misheard!

THE TRADING PIT

Based on copious facts and figures relating to supply and demand, trading in commodity futures is carried on in the same way. These contracts are bought and sold by the brokers on behalf of their clients.

WHAT DOES A 'FUTURE' MEAN?

When you own a commodity future, you effectively hold the right to buy or sell a given commodity at a set price on a specified date in the future.

The commodity must be durable, available in standard-sized lots or units, free from any external controls by governments or producers and essentially international in terms of supply and demand.

Frozen orange juice meets all these requirements. Oranges are primary commodities that are grown in many different parts of the world, the extraction of juice is a process and so the juice becomes an underlying commodity, and finally, the freezing process makes it both durable and measurable.

Agreeing a price and a quantity at a future date reduces the risk of price fluctuation and also ensures supply. This form of price insurance is known as 'hedging'. Both producers and consumers can plan ahead on the basis of a known price and quantity at a given time.

WHAT ARE 'SWAPS' AND 'OPTIONS'?

'Swaps' and 'Options' are refinements to the basic future contract. In a swap, both buyer and seller agree to exchange risks. A buyer may agree to compensate the seller should the market price fall below the price set in the contract.

In turn, the seller may agree to compensate the buyer should the market price rise.

With an option, the buyer pays a fee for the option to pay for a product at the contract price – which is to the buyer's advantage if the market price is higher on the date when the transaction is to take place.

The buyer can also take advantage of the market price on the contract date if they are lower – but in doing so, the buyer forfeits the option fee.

As well as commodity futures there are also Financial Futures and Options. Trading in these financial instruments has rocketed from a little over 20,000 contracts in 1975 to over 100 million a year in 1990.

AND WHAT ARE FUTURES?

Instead of dealing in underlying commodities – Financial Futures mainly deal in interest rate futures, currency futures, and stock index futures.

FINANCIAL FUTURES

The main attraction of any future or derivative is its built-in ability to hedge risks. The US Futures markets in Chicago dominate worldwide Futures and Options trading – with London and Paris gradually catching up.

There are now futures markets in nearly every financial centre in the world – but what is the future? Will it always be about supply and demand – with money and human nature squabbling about in between?

It certainly looks that way. Wealth seems to have travelled full circle. Columbus set off to find the treasures of the East. He found the West instead and now most of America is owned by Japan – in futures!

12

WHO CARES?

THE 'HUBRIDS' ARE COMING!

Since much of modern economics is pure guesswork, based on a few facts and an infinite number of probabilities, you could argue that it has as much to do with *reality* as Science Fiction.

Imagine say, going to see the latest Hollywood Sci-Fi blockbuster film in which the planet is under attack from a dangerous and totally unpredictable alien species whose sole aim is to destroy Earth's capacity for sustaining human life.

Sitting in the dark, maybe holding hands with a friend, we watch as Terrifying Creatures walk the face of the Earth – chopping down trees, blowing up mountains, making deserts, slashing and burning, grabbing money, consuming, and generally destabilizing world economies.

The democratic governments of the Free World are powerless to stop them from saving or investing in whatever they like! It is a nightmare horror movie scenario – even Arnold Schwarzenegger – the Robo-Economist – can do nothing to stop them from taking over the world!

Why? Because these aliens are masters of disguise – they can look and behave like any one of us! In our Science Fiction movie, let us call them – the Hubrids!

Once just ordinary, fallible human beings – only moderately motivated by self-interest and greed – these people have unwittingly become contaminated with *hubris*, an ancient Greek virus – carried by the twentieth-century mass media – that attacks the human mind, convincing an individual that he or she is absolutely right about something – like having to make money – resulting in excessive self-confidence, presumption, pride, arrogance and contempt for any other conflicting opinion.

After a while, the alien virus works in a more subtle way. It reconstructs the human host's vocabulary into dubious metaphors in order to strengthen its arguments – constantly applying the paint of yesterday's ideas to the crumbling walls of tomorrow – compelling the hapless victim to participate in aimless, lengthy and often heated discussions with other Hubrids.

The Hubrids infiltrate governments, banks, multinational corporations, and international money markets – as well as the chattering, muttering, working and thinking classes of today – succeeding only in spreading disinformation, ignorance, muddle and confusion. The human race is doomed!

But never fear! It's only a movie. At last, the house lights come up and the entertainment is over – but what is the economic reality out on the street? What are the economists *really* talking about? How many people really care? Are the Hubrids already here?

AUTHOR'S MESSAGE!

There is far, far more to economics than meets the reader's eye in these humble pages, so it seems only fair that I should offer up some sort of author's message. After all, what do people write books for – surely not just for other people to read? So here I am, and if you will kindly give me a leg up – I shall get on my high horse . . .

In our modern consumer society, money is valued above all because, directly or indirectly, everything else we need has to be bought or sold. We need money in order to possess, consume, or flaunt the things that money can buy.

But what would happen if everyone in the world had enough money to live a life of luxury? If everyone in the world had a private yacht – the oceans would be as crowded as a boating lake in a park and the land would be a virtual desert with everything chopped down or dug up and used to make the yachts.

Nature is red in tooth and claw – there have to be winners and losers – but when (as we are) a species is at the top of the food chain, we have only ourselves to fear. The so-called 'developed' world has tastes and values that are unsustainable without someone else suffering for them.

How long can the notion of sustainable growth keep tempting us with the sort of things we didn't know we wanted until they were so cleverly advertised? How long can we afford to gamble with making money out of money?

Unlike 500 years ago, there is no 'new world' for us to discover – there is nowhere left for us to go. We need to put money to one side – and to think seriously about alternative values if we are to have real quality and meaning in our lives.

The human race has had a great adventure. It has invented many wonderful things of use and value – but at what cost to our home, the planet Earth? Surely it is time to take stock of what we have achieved and to turn this knowledge to our long-term advantage – rather than our downfall.

Do we have to work so hard? All we need to do is supply ourselves with good food, make somewhere comfortable for us to live, and find enjoyable ways of developing our creative and competitive skills that are, for once, in harmony with the rest of nature. Let's keep the best bits and dump the rest!

The *real* wealth of humanity is humanity itself – its children. Man's 'economics' to man has got to change.

History has shown that money has only ever made very few people rich and a very great many thoroughly miserable. There are enough natural disasters in the world each year to occupy us without all the suffering and environmental damage caused by today's extraordinary levels of consumerism.

After all, what is consumerism for? Profits, dividends, getting a return – making money for its own sake. It is like a drug – distorting our perception of reality, our reason, and our sense of responsibility.

Why can't we invest in the Future? Use the money NOW to research, design, manufacture, and employ people to make all the things we KNOW we need – and then educate our children and their children to keep repairing them and maintaining them. No overnight miracles, just a steady, planned, caring and phased programme of withdrawal. If we can send someone to the moon, why can't we do this?

WHO CARES?

We need renewable growth – just like the rest of nature. It is time to kick the profit-making habit, it is making economic halfwits of us all. Let's try and put our house in order and be satisfied with not making a loss for a while. We've had the teenage party, it's time to behave like grown-ups.

Um, . . . if you're still there – I'd like to get down now! I've just noticed hundreds of butterflies on the lavender and I think I'd like to go and look at them for a while . . . I wonder if THEY know anything about the Theory of Chaos . . .?

INDEX OF FINANCIAL TERMS

Each term is defined on the page number given.

Recommended Reading

'ALMOST EVERYONE'S GUIDE TO ECONOMICS'
J.K. Galbraith and Nicole Salinger – Penguin

'APPLIED UK MACROECONOMICS'
Roger Backhouse – Blackwell

'DAWN TRADERS' GUIDE TO WORLD MARKETS'
Robin Amlot – Boxtree

'HOW TO READ THE FINANCIAL PAGES'
Michael Brett – Hutchinson

'MONEY'
Neil Fitzgerald – Blackwell

'WHY ECONOMISTS DISAGREE'
Ken Cole, John Cameron, Chris Edwards – Longman

'THE FEAR OF FREEDOM'
Erich Fromm – Ark Paperbacks

OTHER BOOKS IN PICCADILLY'S 'INFORMATION WITH HUMOUR' SERIES

THE VERY BLOODY HISTORY OF BRITAIN:
Without the Boring Bits
by John Farman
'. . . includes detailed analysis in a chatty narrative style, full of old jokes, which make it immensely readable.'
School Librarian

A SUSPICIOUSLY SIMPLE HISTORY OF SCIENCE AND INVENTION:
Without the Boring Bits
by John Farman
'I found it to be one of the most readable, amusing and informative science books that has come my way for some time . . . Most highly recommended for anyone who wants to put some humour into teaching . . .'
Education Review – NUT

EUROPE UNITED
by Terrance Dicks
'The best Eurobook . . . bright and amusing . . . intelligent and great fun.'
Harry Enfield in The Sunday Times

A RIOT OF WRITERS:
A Romp Through English Literature
by Terrance Dicks
Just published.